Jana Hauschild's Decorative Charted Borders

by Jana Hauschild

DOVER PUBLICATIONS, INC.
New York

Designs copyright © 1990 by Jana Hauschild.
Introduction copyright © 1990 by Dover Publications, Inc.
All rights reserved under Pan American and International Copyright Conventions.

Published in Canada by General Publishing Company, Ltd., 30 Lesmill Road, Don Mills, Toronto, Ontario.
Published in the United Kingdom by Constable and Company, Ltd., 10 Orange Street, London WC2H 7EG.

Jana Hauschild's Decorative Charted Borders is a new work, first published by Dover Publications, Inc., in 1990.

Manufactured in the United States of America
Dover Publications, Inc., 31 East 2nd Street, Mineola, N.Y. 11501

Library of Congress Cataloging-in-Publication Data

Lindberg, Jana Hauschild.
   [Decorative charted borders]
   Jana Hauschild's decorative charted borders / by Jana Hauschild.
      p.   cm. — (Dover needlework series)
   ISBN 0-486-26267-7
   1. Embroidery—Patterns. 2. Knitting—Patterns. 3. Crocheting—Patterns. 4. Borders, Ornamental (Decorative arts) I. Title. II. Title: Decorative charted borders. III. Series.
TT771.L56   1990   89-25882
746.44′041—dc20   CIP

Introduction

Borders and repeat patterns are among the most versatile of all needlework designs. Borders, used in conjunction with other motifs or alone, give the perfect finishing touch to larger projects such as tablecloths or runners, and can also be used for a variety of smaller items such as bookmarks, bellpulls, luggage straps and hatbands. All-over patterns offer an exciting substitute for printed or textured fabrics, enabling you to create one-of-a-kind pillows, tote bags, chair seats, eyeglass cases and much more.

On each of the charts in this book, a section of the design has been marked off and labeled as a "repeat." This means that this section of the chart will be worked over and over until the design is the size desired. Border designs repeat in one direction only, while allover patterns repeat in both directions.

It is best to begin a repeat pattern in the center and work out so that the design is balanced. On some of the designs in the book, the center is marked with a small arrow; on others, the center must be determined. Sometimes there is more than one possible center of a design. For example, the center of a border can fall between two repeats or at the center of the repeat itself.

Many of the borders show one corner of the design. If not, it is very easy to work out the corner with the aid of a small rectangular mirror and some graph paper. Holding the mirror on edge, place it across the chart at a 45° angle. The design will be reflected in the mirror at a right angle and a perfect corner will be formed. Move the mirror along the chart until you find a corner design that you like, then copy it onto the graph paper.

Most of these designs were originally created for counted cross-stitch, but they are easily translated into other needlework techniques. Keep in mind that the finished piece will not be the same size as the charted design unless you are working on fabric or canvas with the same number of threads per inch as the chart has squares per inch. With knitting and crocheting, the size will vary according to the number of stitches per inch.

COUNTED CROSS-STITCH

MATERIALS

1. *Needles.* A small blunt tapestry needle, No. 24 or No. 26.

2. *Fabric.* Evenweave linen, cotton, wool or synthetic fabrics all work well. The most popular fabrics are aida cloth, linen and hardanger cloth. Cotton aida is most commonly available in 18 threads-per-inch, 14 threads-per-inch and 11 threads-per-inch (14-count is the most popular size). Evenweave linen comes in a variety of threads-per-inch. To work cross-stitch on linen involves a slightly different technique (see page 5). Thirty thread-per-inch linen will result in a stitch about the same size as 14-count aida. Hardanger cloth has 22 threads to the inch and is available in cotton or linen. The amount of fabric needed depends on the size of the cross-stitch design. To determine yardage, divide the number of stitches in the design by the thread-count of the fabric. For example: If a design 112 squares wide by 140 squares deep is worked on a 14-count fabric, divide 112 by 14 (= 8), and 140 by 14 (= 10). The design will measure 8″ × 10″. The same design worked on 22-count fabric measures about 5″ × 6½″.

3. *Threads and Yarns.* Six-strand embroidery floss, crewel wool, Danish Flower Thread, pearl cotton or metallic threads all work well for cross-stitch. DMC Embroidery Floss has been used to color-code the patterns in this volume; a conversion chart for Royal Mouliné Six-Strand Embroidery Floss from Coats & Clark, and Anchor Embroidery Floss from Susan Bates appears on page 32. Crewel wool works well on evenweave wool fabric. Danish Flower Thread is a thicker thread with a matte finish, one strand equaling two of embroidery floss.

4. *Embroidery Hoop.* A wooden or plastic 4″, 5″ or 6″ round or oval hoop with a screw-type tension adjuster works best for cross-stitch.

5. *Scissors.* A pair of sharp embroidery scissors is essential to all embroidery.

PREPARING TO WORK

To prevent raveling, either whip stitch or machine-stitch the outer edges of the fabric.

Locate the exact center of the chart. Establish the center of the fabric by folding it in half first vertically, then horizontally. The center stitch of the chart falls where the creases of the fabric meet. Mark the fabric center with a basting thread.

It is best to begin cross-stitch at the top of the design. To establish the top, count the squares up from the center of the chart, and the corresponding number of holes up from the center of the fabric.

Place the fabric tautly in the embroidery hoop, for tension makes it easier to push the needle through the holes without piercing the fibers. While working continue to retighten the fabric as necessary.

When working with multiple strands (such as embroidery floss) always separate (strand) the thread before beginning to stitch. This one small step allows for better coverage of the fabric. When you need more than one thread in the needle, use separate strands and do not double the thread. (For example: If you need four strands, use four separated strands.) Thread has a nap (just as fabrics do) and can be felt to be smoother in one direction than the other. Always work with the nap (the smooth side) pointing down.

For 14-count aida and 30-count linen, work with two strands of six-strand floss. For more texture, use more thread; for a flatter look, use less thread.

EMBROIDERY

To begin, fasten the thread with a waste knot and hold a short length of thread on the underside of the work, anchoring it with the first few stitches *(Diagram 1)*. When the thread end is securely in place, clip the knot.

DIAGRAM 1
Reverse side of work

To stitch, push the needle up through a hole in the fabric, cross the thread intersection (or square) on a left-to-right diagonal *(Diagram 2)*. Half the stitch is now completed.

DIAGRAM 2

Next, cross back, right to left, forming an X *(Diagram 3)*.

DIAGRAM 3   **DIAGRAM 4**

Work all the same color stitches on one row, then cross back, completing the X's *(Diagram 4)*.

Some needleworkers prefer to cross each stitch as they come to it. This method also works, but be sure all of the top stitches are slanted in the same direction. Isolated stitches must be crossed as they are worked. Vertical stitches are crossed as shown in *Diagram 5*.

DIAGRAM 5

At the top, work horizontal rows of a single color, left to right. This method allows you to go from an unoccupied space to an occupied space (working from an empty hole to a filled one), making ruffling of the floss less likely. Holes are used more than once, and all stitches "hold hands" unless a space is indicated on the chart. Hold the work upright throughout (do not turn as with many needlepoint stitches).

When carrying the thread from one area to another, run the needle under a few stitches on the wrong side. Do not carry thread across an open expanse of fabric as it will be visible from the front when the project is completed.

To end a color, weave in and out of the underside of the stitches, making a scallop stitch or two for extra security *(Diagram 6)*. When possible, end in the same direction in which you were working, jumping up a row if necessary *(Diagram 7)*. This prevents holes caused by stitches being pulled in two directions. Trim the thread ends closely and do not leave any tails or knots as they will show through the fabric when the work is completed.

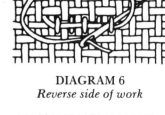

DIAGRAM 6
Reverse side of work

DIAGRAM 7
Reverse side of work

A number of other counted-thread stitches can be used in cross-stitch. Backstitch *(Diagram 8)* is used for outlines, face details and the like. It is worked from hole to hole, and may be stitched as a vertical, horizontal or diagonal line.

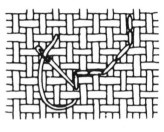

DIAGRAM 8

Straight stitch is worked from side to side over several threads *(Diagram 9)* and affords solid coverage.

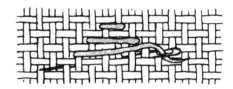

DIAGRAM 9

Lazy daisy stitch *(Diagram 10)* is handy for special effects. It is worked in the same manner as on regular embroidery.

Lazy Daisy Stitch

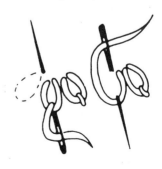

DIAGRAM 10

Embroidery on Linen. Working on linen requires a slightly different technique. While evenweave linen is remarkably regular, there are always a few thick or thin threads. To keep the stitches even, cross-stitch is worked over two threads in each direction *(Diagram 11)*.

DIAGRAM 11

As you are working over more threads, linen affords a greater variation in stitches. A half-stitch can slant in either direction and is uncrossed. A three-quarters stitch is shown in *Diagram 12*.

DIAGRAM 12

Diagram 13 shows the backstitch worked on linen.

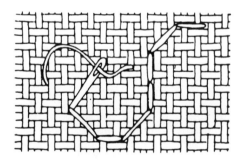

DIAGRAM 13

Embroidery on Gingham. Gingham and other checked fabrics can be used for cross-stitch. Using the fabric as a guide, work the stitches from corner to corner of each check.

Embroidery on Uneven-Weave Fabrics. If you wish to work cross-stitch on an uneven-weave fabric, baste a lightweight Penelope needlepoint canvas to the material. The design can then be stitched by working the cross-stitch over the double mesh of the canvas. When working in this manner, take care not to catch the threads of the canvas in the embroidery. After the cross-stitch is completed, remove the basting threads. With tweezers remove first the vertical threads, one strand at a time, of the needlepoint canvas, then the horizontal threads.

NEEDLEPOINT

One of the most common methods for working needlepoint is from a charted design. By simply viewing each square of a chart as a stitch on the canvas, the patterns quickly and easily translate from one technique to another.

MATERIALS

1. **Needles.** A blunt tapestry needle with a rounded tip and an elongated eye. The needle must clear the hole of the canvas without spreading the threads. For No. 10 canvas, a No. 18 needle works best.

2. **Canvas.** There are two distinct types of needlepoint canvas: single-mesh (mono canvas) and double-mesh (Penelope canvas). Single-mesh canvas, the more common of the two, is easier on the eyes as the spaces are slightly larger. Double-mesh canvas has two horizontal and two vertical threads forming each mesh. The latter is a very stable canvas on which the threads stay securely in place as the work progresses. Canvas is available in many sizes, from 5 mesh-per-inch to 18 mesh-per-inch, and even smaller. The number of mesh-per-inch will, of course, determine the dimensions of the finished needlepoint project. A 60 square × 120 square chart will measure 12″ × 24″ on 5 mesh-to-the-inch canvas, 5″ × 10″ on 12 mesh-to-the-inch canvas. The most common canvas size is 10 to the inch.

3. **Yarns.** Persian, crewel and tapestry yarns all work well on needlepoint canvas.

PREPARING TO WORK

Allow 1″ to 1½″ blank canvas all around. Bind the raw edges of the canvas with masking tape or machine-stitched double-fold bias tape.

There are few hard-and-fast rules on where to begin the design. It is best to complete the main motif, then fill the background as the last step.

For any guidelines you wish to draw on the canvas, take care that your marking medium is waterproof. Non-soluble inks, acrylic paints thinned with water so as not to clog the mesh, and waterproof felt-tip pens all work well. If unsure, experiment on a scrap of canvas.

When working with multiple strands (such as Persian yarn) always separate (strand) the yarn before beginning to stitch. This one small step allows for better coverage of the canvas. When you need more than one piece of yarn in the needle, use separate strands and do not double the yarn. For example: If you need two strands of 3-ply Persian yarn, use two separated strands. Yarn has a nap (just as fabrics do) and can be felt to be smoother in one direction than the other. Always work with the nap (the smooth side) pointing down.

For 5 mesh-to-the-inch canvas, use six strands of 3-ply yarn; for 10 mesh-to-the-inch canvas, use three strands of 3-ply yarn.

STITCHING

Cut yarn lengths 18″ long. Begin needlepoint by holding about 1″ of loose yarn on the wrong side of the work and working the first several stitches over the loose end to secure it. To end a piece of yarn, run it under several completed stitches on the wrong side of the work.

There are hundreds of needlepoint stitch variations, but tent stitch is universally considered to be *the* needlepoint stitch. The most familiar versions of tent stitch are half-cross stitch, continental stitch and basket-weave stitch.

Half-cross stitch *(Diagram 14)* is worked from left to right. The canvas is then turned around and the return row is again stitched from left to right. Holding the needle vertically, bring it to the front of the canvas through the hole that will be the bottom of the first stitch. Keep the stitches loose for minimum distortion and good coverage. Half-cross stitch is best worked on a double-mesh canvas.

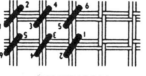

DIAGRAM 14

Continental stitch *(Diagram 15)* begins in the upper right-hand corner and is worked from right to left. The needle is slanted and always brought out a mesh ahead. The resulting stitch appears as a half-cross stitch on the front and as a slanting stitch on the back. When the row is complete, turn the canvas around to work the return row, continuing to stitch from right to left.

DIAGRAM 15

Basket-weave stitch *(Diagram 16)* begins in the upper right-hand corner with four continental stitches (two stitches worked horizontally across the top and two placed directly below the first stitch). Work diagonal rows, the first slanting up and across the canvas from right to left, and the next down and across from left to right. Moving down the canvas from left to right, the needle is in a vertical position; working in the opposite direction, the needle is horizontal. The rows interlock, creating a basket-weave pattern on the wrong side. If the stitch is not done properly, a faint ridge will show where the pattern was interrupted. On basket-weave stitch, always stop working in the middle of a row, rather than at the end, so that you will know in which direction you were working.

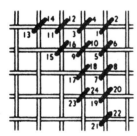

DIAGRAM 16

KNITTING

Charted designs can be worked into stockinette stitch as you are knitting, or they can be embroidered with duplicate stitch when the knitting is complete. For the former, wind the different colors of yarn on bobbins and work in the same manner as in Fair Isle knitting. A few quick Fair Isle tips: (1) Always bring up the new color yarn from under the dropped color to prevent holes. (2) Carry the color not in use loosely across the wrong side of the work, but not more than three or four stitches without twisting the yarns. If a color is not in use for more than seven or eight stitches, it is usually best to drop that color yarn and rejoin a new bobbin when the color is again needed.

CROCHET

There are a number of ways in which charts can be used for crochet. Among them are:

SINGLE CROCHET

Single crochet is often seen worked in multiple colors. When changing colors, always pick up the new color for the last yarn-over of the old color. The color not in use can be carried loosely across the back of the work for a few stitches, or you can work the single crochet over the unused color. The latter method makes for a neater appearance on the wrong side, but sometimes the old color peeks through the stitches. This method can also be applied to half-double crochet and double crochet, but keep in mind that the longer stitches will distort the design.

FILET CROCHET

This technique is nearly always worked from charts and uses only one color thread. The result is a solid-color piece with the design filled in and the background left as an open mesh. Care must be taken in selecting the design, as the longer stitch causes distortion.

AFGHAN CROCHET

The most common method here is cross-stitch worked over the afghan stitch. Complete the afghan crochet project. Then, following the chart for color placement, work cross-stitch over the squares of crochet.

OTHER CHARTED METHODS

Latch hook, Assisi embroidery, beading, cross-stitch on needlepoint canvas (a European favorite) and lace net embroidery are among the other needlework methods worked from charts.

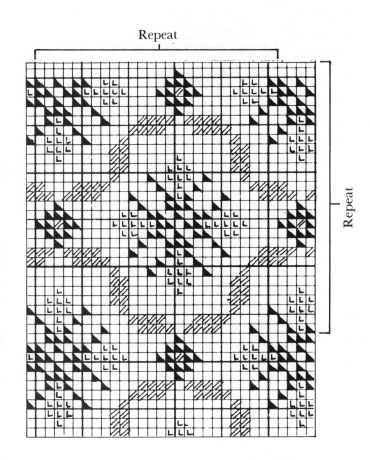

DMC #

◨	702	Kelly Green
L	893	Light Carnation Red
╱	907	Light Parrot Green

This is an allover pattern.

▼ **DMC #**

◨	304	Medium Christmas Red
╱	320	Medium Pistachio Green
X	581	Moss Green
·	725	Topaz
●	730	Very Dark Olive Green
I	833	Medium Golden Wheat
L	3328	Medium Salmon
■	3345	Dark Hunter Green

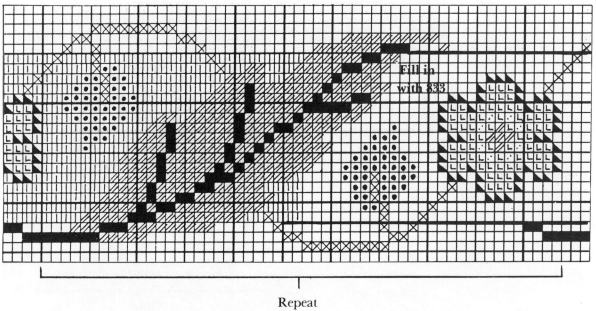

Back-stitch	Cross-stitch	DMC #	
—	■	356	Medium Terra-cotta
	∧	471	Light Avocado Green
	⊙	581	Moss Green

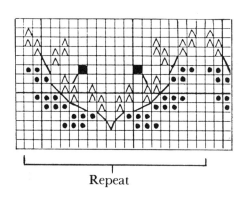

Repeat

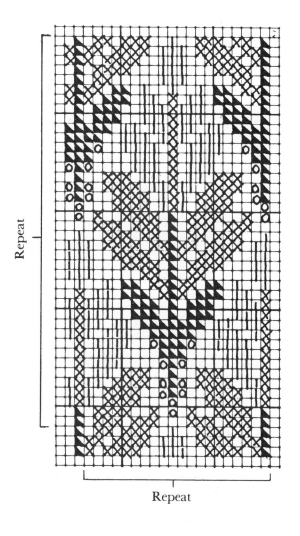

Repeat

	DMC #	
⊠	730	Very Dark Olive Green
⌶	733	Medium Olive Green
□	834	Light Golden Wheat (background)
◣	936	Very Dark Avocado Green
⊙	977	Light Golden Brown

This is an allover pattern.

Back-stitch	Cross-stitch	DMC #	
	◣	904	Very Dark Parrot Green
	╱	906	Medium Parrot Green
—		907	Light Parrot Green
	⊙		White

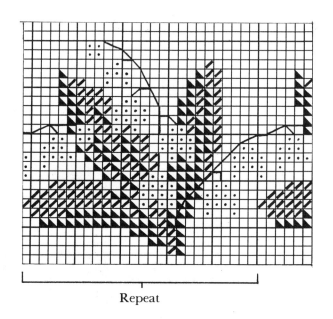

Repeat

▼ **Back-stitch**	**Cross-stitch**	**DMC #**
	⊙	798	Dark Delft Blue
	L	799	Medium Delft Blue
—		3046	Light Yellow Beige
	⊠	3347	Medium Yellow Green

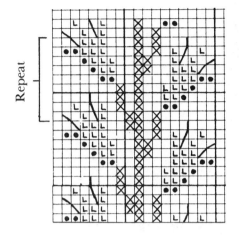

▼ **Back-stitch**	**Cross-stitch**	**DMC #**
	⊠	444	Dark Lemon Yellow
	◣	904	Very Dark Parrot Green
	╱	905	Dark Parrot Green
	∧	906	Medium Parrot Green
	L	907	Light Parrot Green
—	⊙	972	Yellow Orange
	∴		White

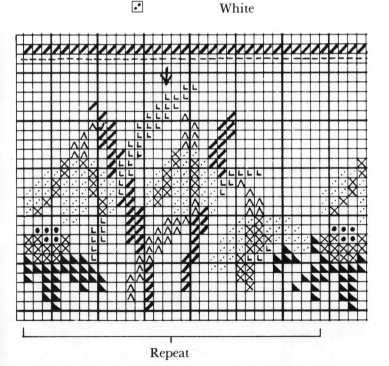

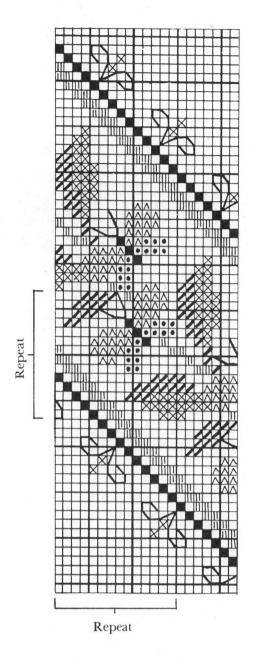

Back-stitch	**Cross-stitch**	**DMC #** ▲
	⊠	581	Moss Green
	╱	730	Very Dark Olive Green
	⊙	792	Dark Cornflower Blue
	∧	793	Medium Cornflower Blue
—	■	3021	Dark Brown Gray
	‖	3045	Dark Yellow Beige

When working this diagonal border, be sure to move the design up by 14 stitches on each repeat, as well as over, so that the design is continuous.

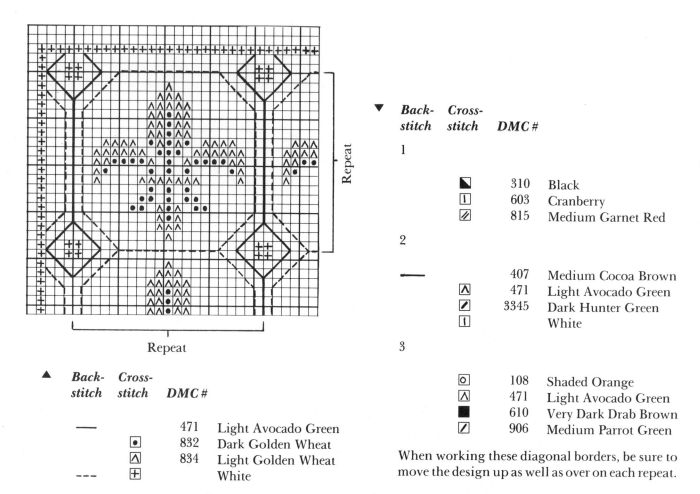

▼ Back- Cross-
stitch stitch DMC #

1

■ 310 Black
| 603 Cranberry
⁄ 815 Medium Garnet Red

2

— 407 Medium Cocoa Brown
∧ 471 Light Avocado Green
⁄ 3345 Dark Hunter Green
| White

3

○ 108 Shaded Orange
∧ 471 Light Avocado Green
■ 610 Very Dark Drab Brown
⁄ 906 Medium Parrot Green

When working these diagonal borders, be sure to move the design up as well as over on each repeat.

▲ Back- Cross-
stitch stitch DMC #

— 471 Light Avocado Green
• 832 Dark Golden Wheat
∧ 834 Light Golden Wheat
--- + White

This is an allover pattern.

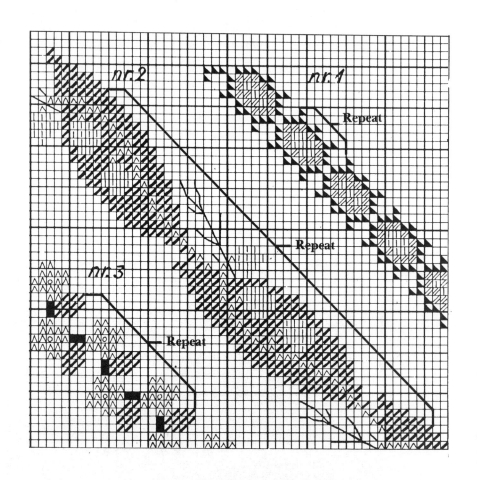

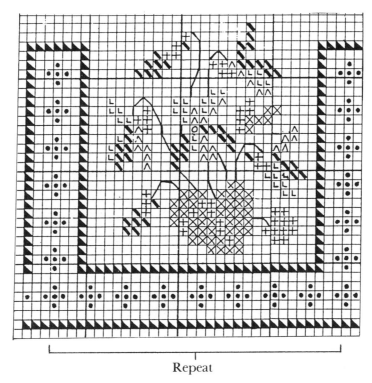

Repeat

Back-stitch	Cross-stitch	DMC #	
	◣	208	Very Dark Lavender
	∧	209	Dark Lavender
	L	210	Medium Lavender
	◣	414	Dark Steel Gray
—	+	471	Light Avocado Green
	X	581	Moss Green
	○	741	Medium Tangerine
	●	832	Dark Golden Wheat

Back-stitch	Cross-stitch	DMC #	
	●	603	Cranberry
---	∧	604	Light Cranberry
	◣	731	Dark Olive Green
—	X	906	Medium Parrot Green
∼∼	L	907	Light Parrot Green

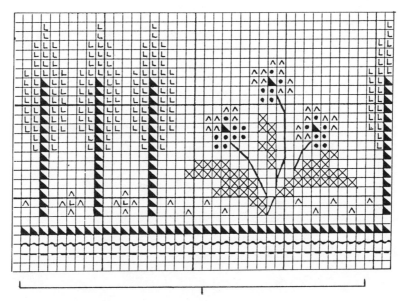

Repeat

11

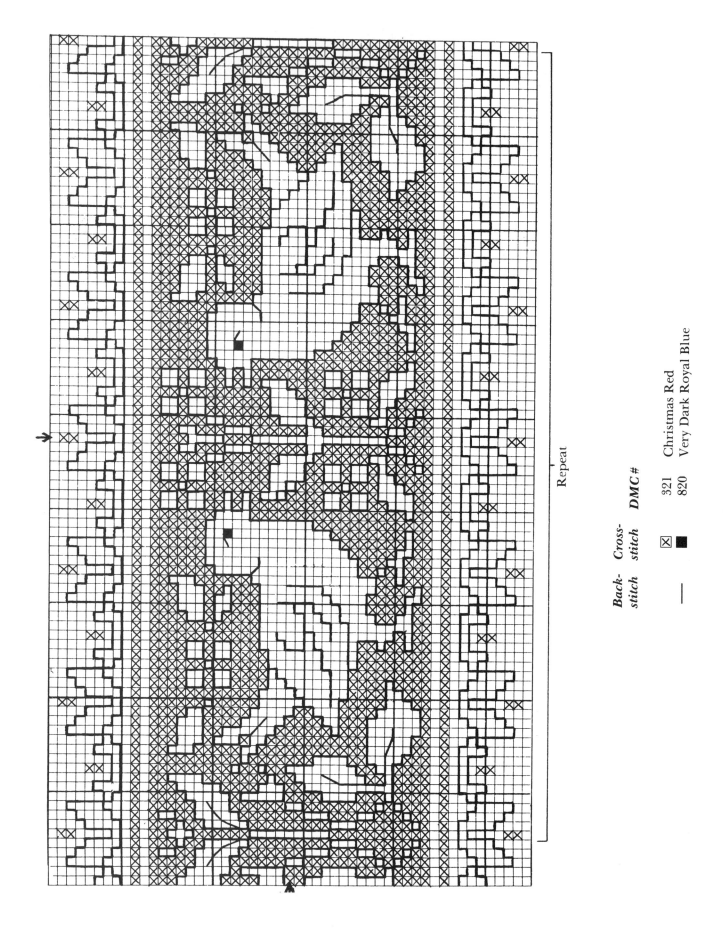

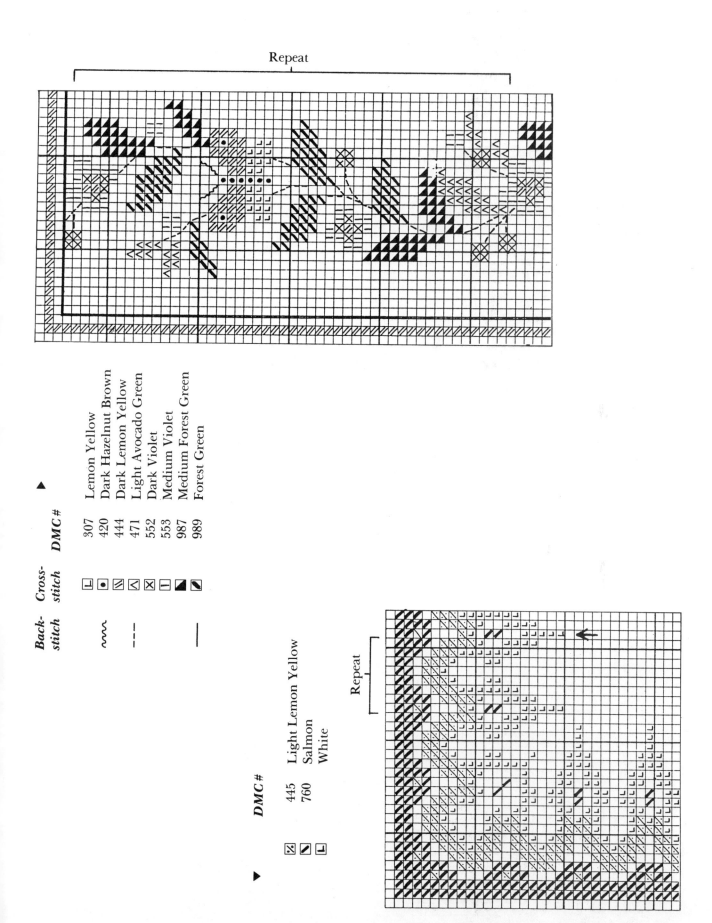

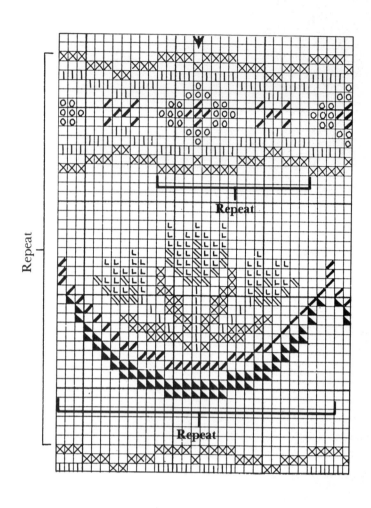

	DMC #	
☒	580	Dark Moss Green
∐	581	Moss Green
o	725	Topaz
L	760	Salmon
╱	782	Medium Topaz
◣	830	Medium Greenish Brown
◪	3328	Medium Salmon

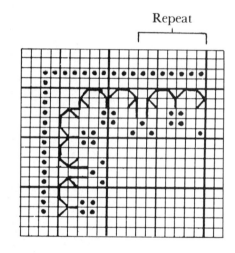

Back-stitch	Cross-stitch	DMC #	
—	⊡	921	Copper

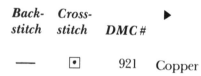

Back-stitch	Cross-stitch	DMC #	
········		581	Moss Green
----	⊞	741	Medium Tangerine
	⊡	921	Copper

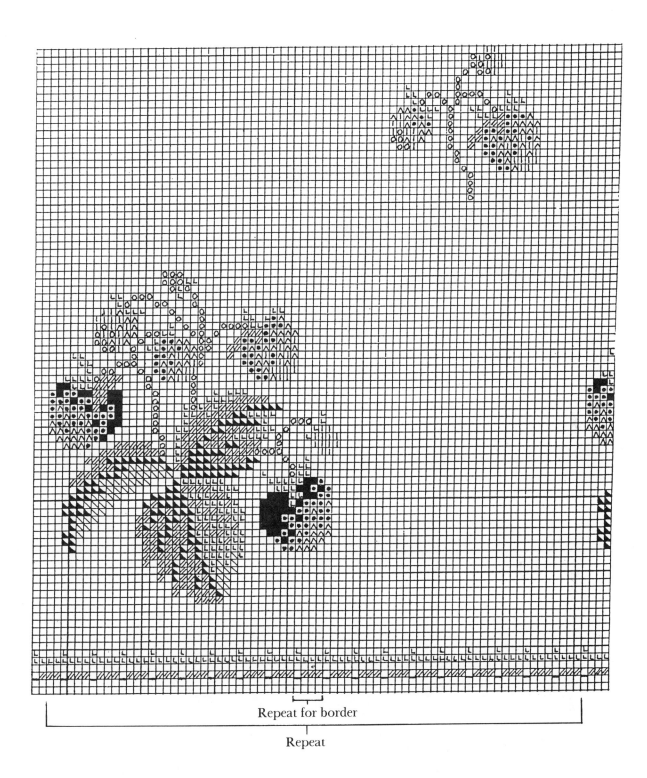

Repeat for border

Repeat

▲	DMC #	
■	321	Christmas Red
∧	351	Coral
○	471	Light Avocado Green
◣	563	Medium Sea Foam Green
•	606	Bright Orange Red
L	703	Chartreuse
I	758	Light Terra-cotta
∕∕	905	Dark Parrot Green
◨	986	Dark Forest Green

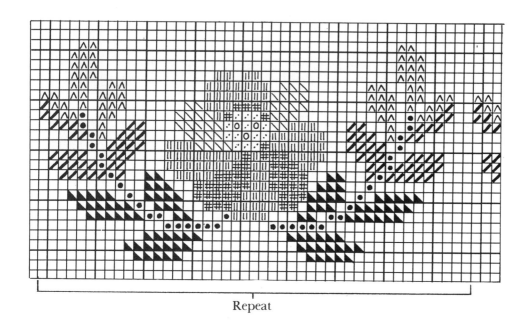

	DMC #	▲	
⌗	309	Deep Rose	
⋅	445	Light Lemon Yellow	
O	725	Topaz	
●	831	Light Greenish Brown	
∥	893	Light Carnation	
╲	894	Very Light Carnation	
◣	904	Very Dark Parrot Green	
╱	906	Medium Parrot Green	
∧	907	Light Parrot Green	

	DMC #	▶	
◣	732	Olive Green	
●	970	Dark Golden Brown	
L	972	Yellow Orange	
✕	988	Forest Green	

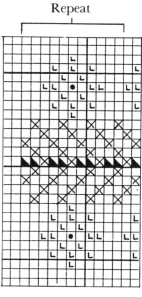

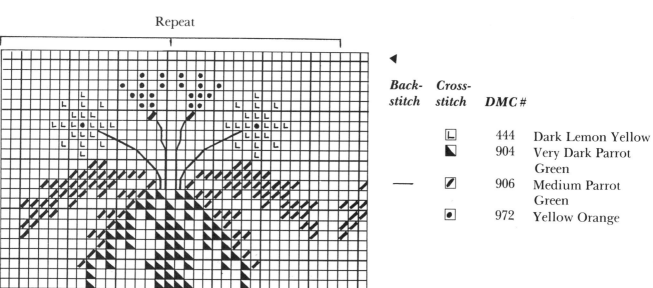

Back-stitch	Cross-stitch	DMC #	
	L	444	Dark Lemon Yellow
	◣	904	Very Dark Parrot Green
—	╱	906	Medium Parrot Green
	●	972	Yellow Orange

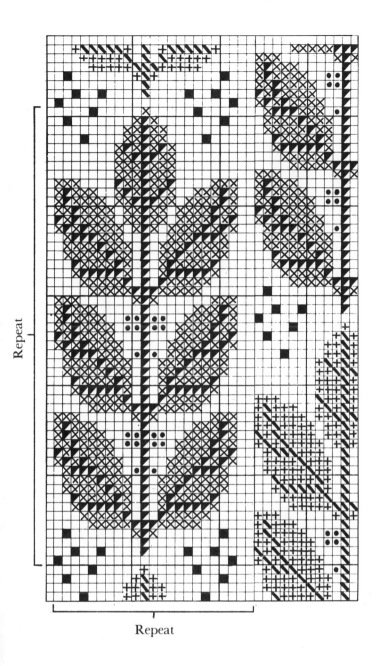

▲ *DMC #*

■	400	Dark Mahogany
✚	471	Light Avocado Green
◪	680	Dark Old Gold
◩	733	Medium Olive Green
✕	734	Light Olive Green
⊙	900	Dark Burnt Orange

This is an allover pattern. The basic motif is the same throughout; however, the colors alternate and each column of motifs is shifted up half a motif.

▼ *DMC #*

◪	309	Deep Rose
I	353	Peach
L	470	Medium Light Avocado Green
■	815	Medium Garnet Red
⊙	831	Light Greenish Brown
∧	893	Light Carnation
◣	986	Dark Forest Green
III	988	Forest Green

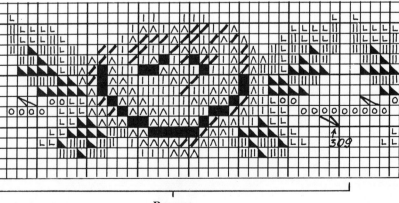

17

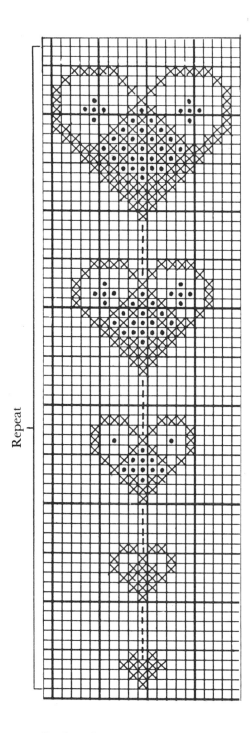

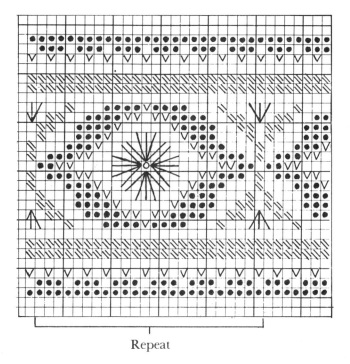

▲ **Back- Cross-**
stitch stitch DMC #

—		349	Dark Coral
	ⱽ	420	Dark Hazelnut Brown
	⊙	725	Topaz
	⊠	991	Dark Aquamarine
	●	3371	Black Brown

▼ **DMC #**

∿∿	368	Light Pistachio Green
—	433	Medium Brown
......	760	Salmon
- - -	834	Light Golden Wheat

This allover pattern is worked entirely in backstitch. The design is bordered by a row of medallions and filled in with a grid of backstitch squares.

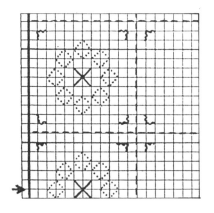

▲ **Back- Cross-**
stitch stitch DMC #

	⊠	White
- - -	⊡	Metallic Gold

This pattern looks best if the repeats are widely spaced.

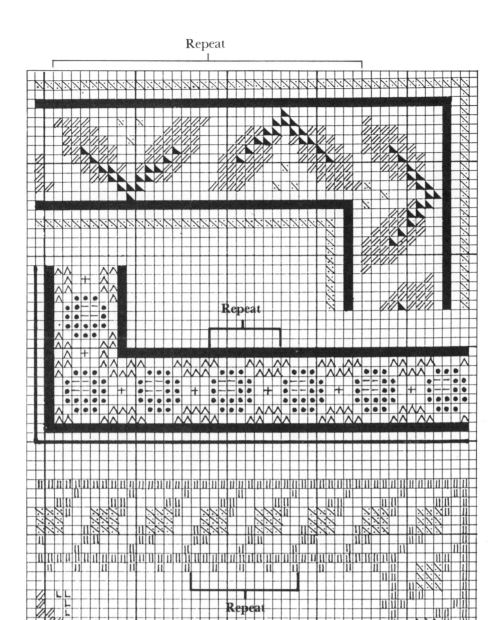

	Back-stitch	Cross-stitch	DMC #	
		N	351	Coral
		+	444	Dark Lemon Yellow
		L	471	Light Avocado Green
		•	798	Dark Delft Blue
		–	809	Delft Blue
		‖	817	Very Dark Coral
		■	831	Light Greenish Brown
		∧	954	Nile Green
	—	◣	987	Medium Forest Green
		∕∕	989	Forest Green

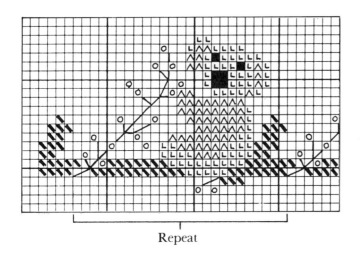

Repeat

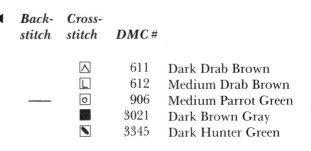

Back-stitch	Cross-stitch	DMC #	
	∧	611	Dark Drab Brown
	L	612	Medium Drab Brown
—	o	906	Medium Parrot Green
	■	3021	Dark Brown Gray
	◣	3345	Dark Hunter Green

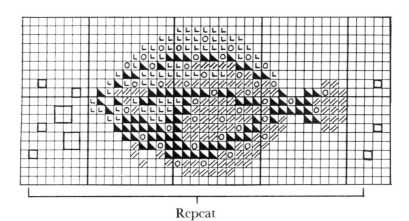

Repeat

▲ Back-stitch Cross-stitch DMC #

	◣	610	Very Dark Drab Brown
	L	612	Medium Drab Brown
—		807	Peacock Blue
	∕	831	Light Greenish Brown
	⊙	976	Medium Golden Brown

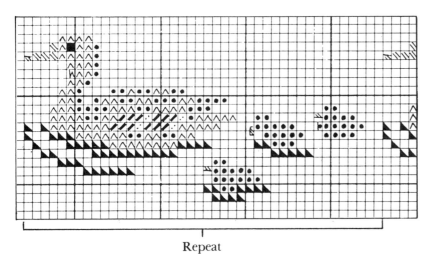

Repeat

◀ DMC #

■	310	Black
⊙	610	Very Dark Drab Brown
∕	792	Dark Cornflower Blue
∖	977	Light Golden Brown
◣	991	Dark Aquamarine
∧	3032	Medium Mocha Brown
·		White

Repeat

This design was originally worked on linen and a few of the stitches were worked over 2 threads only.

DMC # ▶

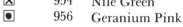 518 Light Wedgwood Blue
✗ 954 Nile Green
⊙ 956 Geranium Pink

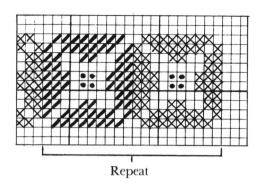

Repeat

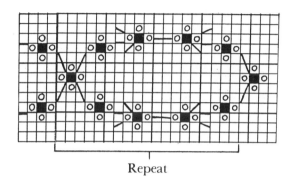

Repeat

◀ *Back-   Cross-*
   stitch   stitch   DMC #

■ 420 Dark Hazelnut Brown
—   906 Medium Parrot Green
   ⊙ 972 Yellow Orange

Repeat

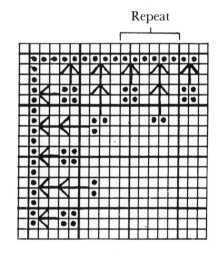

Back-   Cross-
stitch   stitch   DMC # ▶

—   ⊙   702   Kelly Green

Repeat

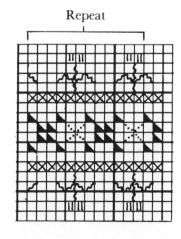

◀ *Back-   Cross-*
   stitch   stitch   DMC #

  ◣   553   Medium Violet
∼∼   ‖   815   Medium Garnet Red
      ✗   907   Light Parrot Green
·······   972   Yellow Orange

21

Use any color desired.
We used 347 Dark Salmon.

DMC # ▶

⊡	93	Shaded Blue
⊙	783	Christmas Gold
☐	898	Very Dark Coffee Brown (for background)
⊠		Metallic Gold

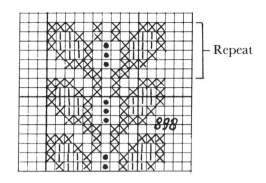

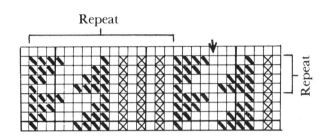

◀ **DMC #**

◨	898	Very Dark Coffee Brown
⊠	975	Dark Golden Brown

DMC # ▶

◣	310	Black
L	893	Light Carnation
⊠	917	Medium Plum

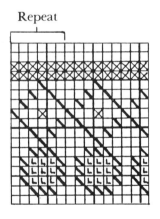

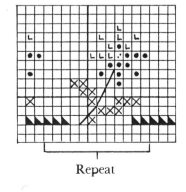

Repeat

◀ **Back-stitch** **Cross-stitch** **DMC #**

Back-stitch	Cross-stitch	DMC #	
	⊡	444	Dark Lemon Yellow
——	◣	580	Dark Moss Green
	⊙	602	Medium Cranberry
	L	956	Geranium Pink
	⊠	989	Light Forest Green

24

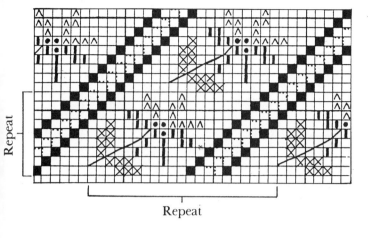

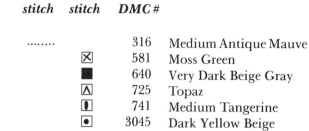

Back-stitch	Cross-stitch	DMC #	
....		316	Medium Antique Mauve
	⊠	581	Moss Green
	■	640	Very Dark Beige Gray
	∧	725	Topaz
	◐	741	Medium Tangerine
	•	3045	Dark Yellow Beige

When working this diagonal border, be sure to move the design up as well as over on each repeat. This design can also be worked as an allover pattern.

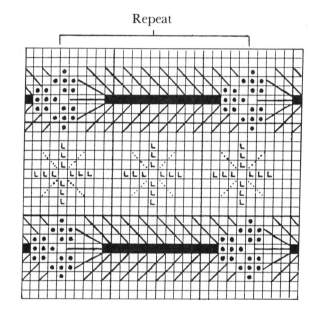

Back-stitch	Cross-stitch	DMC #	▶
	•	606	Bright Orange Red
	■	830	Medium Greenish Brown
—		905	Dark Parrot Green
....	L	972	Yellow Orange

◀ **DMC #**

⊠	606	Bright Orange Red
◐	906	Medium Parrot Green
•		Metallic Gold

25

Repeat

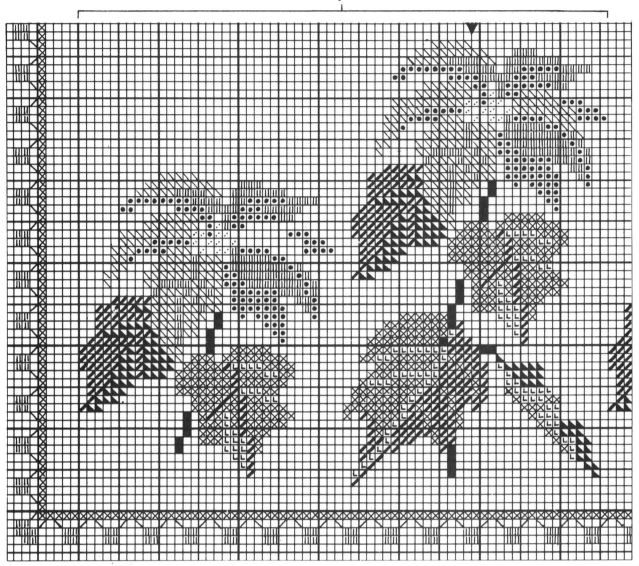

DMC #

Symbol	Number	Name
III	350	Medium Coral
◨	351	Coral
■	407	Medium Cocoa Brown
L	471	Light Avocado Green
∴	725	Topaz
●	817	Very Dark Coral
◤	986	Dark Forest Green
◢	988	Forest Green
⊠	3347	Medium Yellow Green

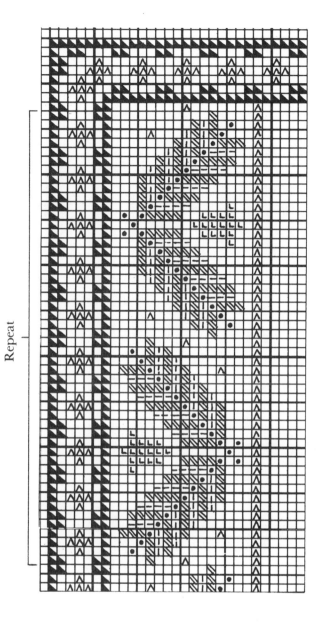

◀ Back- Cross-
stitch stitch DMC #

	⋀	606	Bright Orange Red
	●	680	Dark Old Gold
	⧅	906	Medium Parrot Green
	◼	911	Medium Emerald Green
---	L		Metallic Gold

Use 2 strands of gold thread for cross-stitches and 1 strand for backstitches.

DMC # ▶

I	350	Medium Coral
L	471	Light Avocado Green
●	581	Moss Green
⋀	817	Very Dark Coral
◼	986	Dark Forest Green
⧅	988	Forest Green

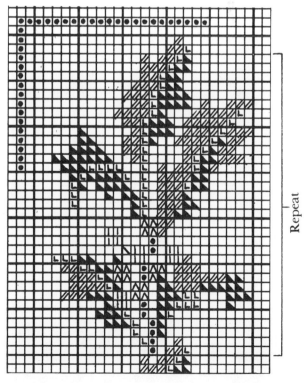

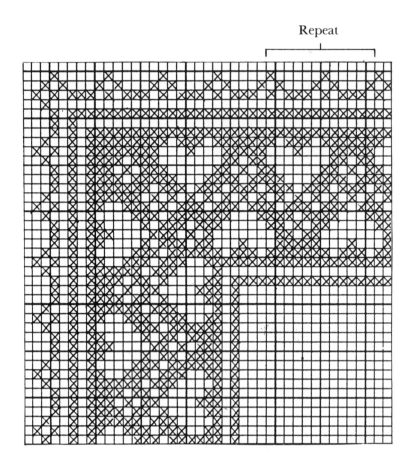

▶		*DMC #*	
	⊠	606	Bright Orange Red

Back-stitch	Cross-stitch	DMC #	▶
—	◣	420	Dark Hazelnut Brown
	⊙	817	Very Dark Coral
	⧄	905	Dark Parrot Green
	⊠	946	Medium Burnt Orange
	L	972	Yellow Orange

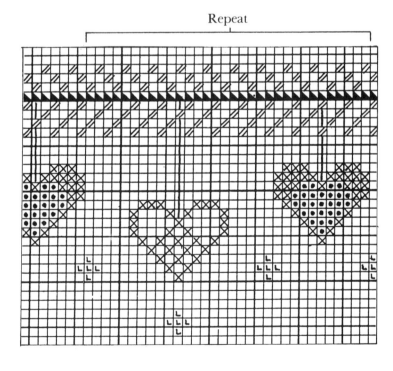

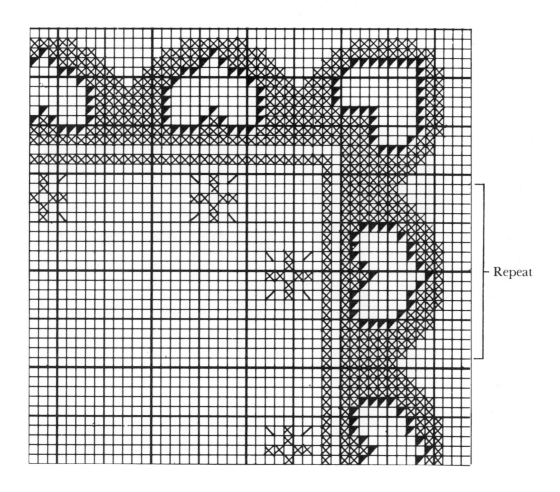

Back-stitch	Cross-stitch	DMC #
—	☒	White
	◣	Metallic Gold

This design should be worked on colored fabric.

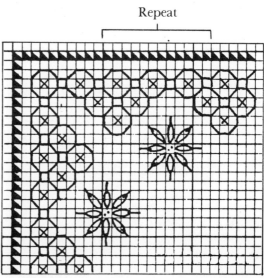

Lazy daisy stitch	Back-stitch	Cross-stitch	DMC #	
Blues				
		⊡	734	Light Olive Green
	—	◣	797	Royal Blue
◊		☒	799	Medium Delft Blue
Reds				
		⊡	445	Light Lemon Yellow
	—	◣	3687	Mauve
◊		☒	3688	Medium Light Mauve

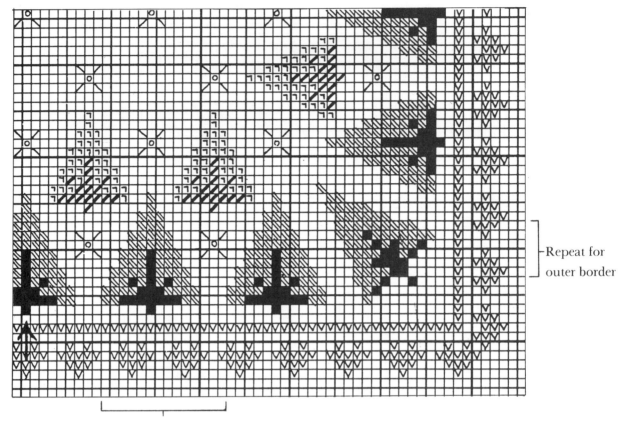

Repeat for outer border

Repeat for tree design

	Back-stitch	Cross-stitch	DMC #	
		V	350	Medium Coral
		■	501	Dark Blue Green
		◩	703	Chartreuse
		⌐	907	Light Parrot Green
		╱	988	Forest Green
	—	o		Metallic Gold

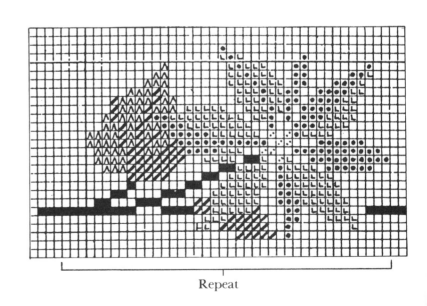

DMC #	▶	
•	349	Dark Coral
L	351	Coral
■	420	Dark Hazelnut Brown
⋅	725	Topaz
╱	987	Medium Forest Green
∧	3347	Medium Yellow Green

Repeat

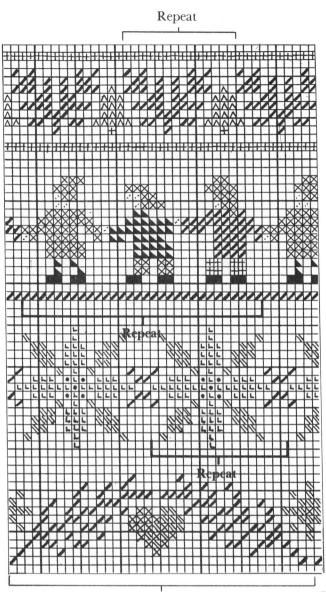

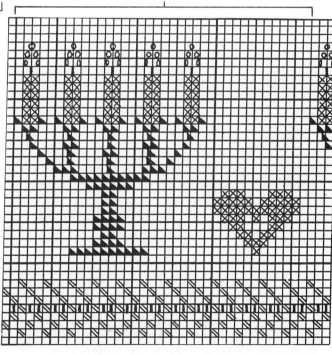

	DMC #	
■	310	Black
ʌ	519	Sky Blue
╱	562	Sea Foam Green
X	606	Bright Orange Red
∴	754	Light Peach
◣	797	Royal Blue
✚	832	Dark Golden Wheat
●	971	Pumpkin
◥	972	Yellow Orange
L	973	Bright Canary Yellow

	DMC #	
◣	310	Black
X	321	Christmas Red
◥	701	Light Christmas Green
❙	831	Light Greenish Brown
o	972	Yellow Orange

This design is best worked on linen, since some of the stitches are moved over by a half a square.

31

SIX STRAND EMBROIDERY COTTON (FLOSS) CONVERSION CHART

KEY: T = Possible Substitute   * = Close Match   — = No Match

DMC NO.	ROYAL MOULINÉ NO.	BATES/ANCHOR NO.
White	1001	2
Ecru	8600	926
208	3335*	110*
209	3415*	105
210	3320*	104
211	3410	108*
221	2570	897*
223	2555	894
224	2545	893
225	2540	892
300	8330	352*
301	8315*	349*
304	2415*	47*
307	6005*	289*
309	2525*	42*
310	1002	403
311	4275T	149*
312	—	147*
315	3130	896*
316	3120	895*
317	1030*	400*
318	1020*	399*
319	5025	246*
320	5015	216*
321	2415	47
322	—	978*
326	2530*	59*
327	3365*	101*
333	—	119
334	4250T	145
335	2525T	42*
336	4270*	149*
340	—	118
341	—	117
347	2425*	13*
349	2400	13
350	2045T	11
351	2015T	11*
352	2015	10*
353	2010*	8*
355	8095	5968
356	8090	5975*
367	5020	216*
368	5005*	240*
369	5005	213*
370	—	889*
371	—	888*
372	—	887*
400	8325*	351
402	8305*	347*
407	8005	882*
413	1025*	401
414	1020*	400*
415	1015	398
420	8720*	375*
422	8710*	373*
433	8265	371*
434	8215	309
435	8210*	369*
436	8205	363*

DMC NO.	ROYAL MOULINÉ NO.	BATES/ANCHOR NO.
437	8200*	362
444	6155*	291
445	6000	288
451	—	399*
452	—	399*
453	1015T	397*
469	5255	267*
470	5255*	267
471	5245	266*
472	5240	264*
498	2425T	20*
500	5125	879*
501	5120*	878
502	5110	876
503	5105	875
504	5100	213*
517	4860*	169*
518	4855T	168*
519	—	167*
520	—	862*
522	—	859*
523	—	859*
524	—	858*
535	1115T	401*
543	8500	933*
550	3380*	102*
552	3370*	101
553	3360	98
554	3355*	96*
561	—	212*
562	—	210*
563	—	208*
564	—	203*
580	5935	267*
581	5925	266*
597	4860*	168*
598	4855*	167*
600	2225*	59*
601	2225*	78*
602	2640*	77*
603	2720*	76*
604	2710	75*
605	2155	50*
606	7260	335
608	7255	333*
610	58251	889*
611	5735T	898
612	8815*	832
613	5605*	956*
632	8530	936*
640	8625	903
642	8620*	392
644	8800	830
645	1115	905*
646	1115*	8581
647	1110	8581*
648	1100*	900
666	2405	46
676	6250	891
677	—	886*

DMC NO.	ROYAL MOULINÉ NO.	BATES/ANCHOR NO.
680	6260*	901
699	5375	923*
700	5365*	229
701	5365*	227
702	5330	239
703	5320	238
704	5310*	256*
712	8600*	387*
718	3015*	88
720	—	326
721	—	324*
722	—	323*
725	6215	306*
726	6150*	295
727	6135	293
729	6255	890
730	—	924*
731	—	281*
732	5925T	281*
733	—	280*
734	—	279*
738	8245*	942
739	8240*	885*
740	7045	316
741	6125	304
742	6120	303
743	6210	297
744	6110*	301*
745	6105	300*
746	6100	386*
747	4850	158*
754	8075	778*
758	8080	868
760	2035	9*
761	2030	8*
762	1010*	397
772	—	264*
775	4600*	128*
776	2110*	24*
778	3110	968*
780	8215*	310*
781	8215	309*
782	6230	308
783	6220*	307
791	4165*	941*
792	4155T	940
793	4155	121
794	4145	120*
796	4340	133*
797	4265*	132*
798	4325	131*
799	4250*	130*
800	4310	128
801	8405	357*
806	4870T	169*
807	4860*	168*
809	4145*	130*
813	4610T	160*
814	2340T	44*
815	2530*	43

DMC NO.	ROYAL MOULINÉ NO.	BATES/ANCHOR NO.
816	2530	44*
817	2415T	19
818	2505*	48
819	2000	892*
820	4345	134
822	8605*	387*
823	4400*	150
824	4225	164*
825	4215	162*
826	4210	161*
827	4605	159*
828	4850	158*
829	5825	906
830	5825*	889*
831	5825T	889*
832	5815	907
833	5815*	874*
834	5810*	874
838	8425*	380
839	8560	380*
840	8555	379*
841	8550	378*
842	8505	376*
844	1115T	401*
869	8720*	944*
890	5025*	879*
891	2135	35*
892	2130	28
893	2125T	27
894	2115T	26
895	5430	246*
898	8425*	243*
899	2515	27*
900	7230*	333
902	—	72*
904	5295*	258*
905	5295	258*
906	5285*	256*
907	5280*	255
909	5370	229*
910	5370*	228*
911	5465*	205*
912	5465	205
913	5460*	209
915	3030	89*
917	3020*	89*
918	8330*	341*
919	8095*	341*
920	8060*	339*
921	8060T	349*
922	8315T	324*
924	4830T	851*
926	4820*	779*
927	4810T	849*
928	1010T	900*
930	4510	922*
931	4505	921*
932	4500	920*
934	5070T	862*
935	5225T	862*

DMC NO.	ROYAL MOULINÉ NO.	BATES/ANCHOR NO.
936	5260T	269
937	5260	268
938	8430	381
939	4405	127
943	4935*	188*
945	8020*	347*
946	7230*	332*
947	7255*	330*
948	8070	778*
950	8020T	4146
951	8020T	366*
954	5455*	203*
955	5450	206*
956	2170*	40*
957	2160T	40*
958	—	187
959	—	186
961	2515*	76*
962	2515	76*
963	2505	49*
964	—	185
966	5150*	214*
970	7040	316*
971	7045	316*
972	6120*	298
973	6015	290
975	8365	355*
976	8355	308*
977	8350	307*
986	5430	246*
987	5020T	244*
988	5295T	243*
989	5405T	242*
991	5165T	189*
992	4925*	187*
993	4915*	186*
995	4710	410
996	4700	433
3011	5525T	845*
3012	5525*	844
3013	5515	842*
3021	5430	382*
3022	—	8581*
3023	—	8581*
3024	1100	900*
3031	—	905*
3032	8620T	903*
3033	8610*	388*
3041	3215*	871
3042	3205*	869
3045	6260T	373*
3046	5810	887*
3047	5805	886*
3051	5530T	846*
3052	5060T	859*
3053	5055*	859*
3064	8005*	914*
3072	4805*	397*
3078	6130	292*
3325	4200	159*

DMC NO.	ROYAL MOULINÉ NO.	BATES/ANCHOR NO.
3326	2115*	25*
3328	2045	11*
3340	—	329
3341	—	328
3345	5025T	268*
3346	5220T	257*
3347	5210*	266*
3348	5270*	265
3350	2220	42*
3354	2210	74*
3362	—	862*
3363	—	861*
3364	—	843*
3371	8435	382
3607	—	87*
3608	—	86
3609	—	85
3685	2335	70*
3687	2325	69*
3688	2320	66*
3689	2310	49
3705	—	35*
3706	—	28*
3708	—	26*
48	9000*	1201*
51	9014	1220
52	9006	1208
53	—	—
57	9002	1203
61	9013T	1218*
62	9000T	1208*
67	—	1211*
69	—	1218*
75	9002	1206*
90	9012T	1217*
91	9008*	1211
92	9011T	1216*
93	9007*	1210*
94	9011*	1216
95	9006T	1208*
99	9005T	1207*
101	9009*	1213*
102	—	1208*
103	—	1211*
104	9012	1217
105	9013T	1218
106	9002T	1203*
107	9003	1204
108	9014*	1220*
111	—	1218*
112	9003T	1204*
113	9007*	1210*
114	9010	1215
115	9004	1206
121	9007	1210
122	9010T	1215*
123	—	1213*
124	9007T	1210*
125	9009	1213
126	9006*	1208*